Windows® 10 Introduction

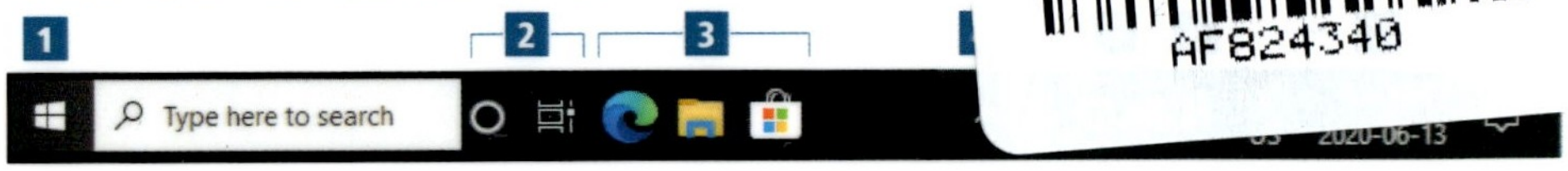

Getting Started

Throughout this guide, where we use [Click], [Right Click], and [Double Click], you can use the touch equivalents of [Tap], [Press and Hold], and [Double Tap]. See **Mouse/ Touch Equivalents**.

Starting Windows

1. [Click] or [Swipe Up] the starting picture.
2. If necessary, select a user.
3. Sign in with your last-used method.

- Sign-in methods include typing a password then pressing <Enter> or [Clicking] ; typing a PIN; gestures on a picture; or scanning fingerprint, face, or iris.
- For password or PIN sign-in [Click] to temporarily see what you've typed.
- If you have set up alternative sign-in methods (see **Configuring Sign-In**), switch among them by [Clicking] SIGN-IN OPTIONS and selecting:
  - – Picture password.
  - – Typed password.
  - – PIN password.
- Sync settings across all your Windows 10 devices by using the same sign-in. See **Using the Settings App** to configure this behavior.

Ending Your Windows Session

End a computing session by locking your screen, signing out, or shutting the device down.

- **To lock your screen:** [Click] , your account picture , then choose LOCK. Or, press <-L>.
- **To unlock your screen:** [Swipe up] or [Click] anywhere on the screen, then sign in.
- **To sign out:** [Click] , your account picture , and choose SIGN OUT.
- **To sleep, shut down, or restart your device:** [Click] then , then select an option.

Accessing Apps and Content (Start Menu) 1

[Click] in lower left, or press the Windows key <> to access the Start menu. On the left is an app list, and on the right, a pane of app tiles. The left side list includes:

- – The menu expander at the top.
- – Your account: Change account settings, Lock your device, Sign Out or switch to another user.
- – Documents: Opens the Documents folder.
- – Downloads: Opens the Downloads folder.
- – File Explorer: To access your documents and files.
- – Settings: To access most settings for Windows.

- There is an alphabetical list of installed apps, but searching may be easier (see **Searching for Apps**).
- [Right Click] the Start menu button , or press <-X> to access power user tools.

Configuring the Start Menu

[Click] , then , PERSONALIZATION, START.

- Turn on/off SHOW MORE TILES ON START to add/ remove a fourth column of medium tiles.
- Turn on/off SHOW SUGGESTIONS OCCASIONALLY IN START to enable/disable display of Start menu ads.
- Turn on/off the Most Used or Recently Added app lists.
- Turn on/off the ability to display Jump Lists (Recently Used Files, Common Tasks) for pinned apps in both the Start menu and on the Taskbar.
- [Click] CHOOSE WHICH FOLDERS APPEAR ON START to add or remove pinned folders (e.g., File Explorer, Settings).

Rearranging and Resizing App Tiles

- [Drag] a tile to a new position within the tile group or [Drag] the group title bar to rearrange the group.
- [Right Click] a tile, choose RESIZE, then select a size.

Resizing the Start Menu

1. [Hover] over the top or right edges of the Start menu. The mouse pointer changes to a double-headed arrow, .
2. [Drag] the edge.

Pinning an App Tile to Start

1. [Right Click] any app on the Desktop, or within the Start app list or, with File Explorer, an app or folder.
2. Select PIN TO START.

To remove an app tile, [Right Click] the tile and select UNPIN FROM START.

Managing Tile Groups

Create a new group by [Dragging] a tile onto another tile.

Naming a Tile Group:

1. [Hover] just above the tile group, then [Click] NAME GROUP.
2. Type the name, then press <Enter>.

To remove a name, [Click] on the name then [Click] .

Accessing Apps and Notifications (Taskbar)

Taskbar icons (vary according to installed hardware):

1 **Start menu button:** Access apps and content
2 **System:** Cortana, Task View
3 **Pinned Apps:** Edge, File Explorer, Store
4 **System Tray:** Icons for apps running in the background
5 **Hardware Status Indicators:** Battery, WiFi, Sound
6 **Windows Security:** Default anti-virus program
7 **Miscellaneous:** Touch Keyboard, Date/Time, Action Center.

Configuring the Taskbar

[Right Click] a blank spot on the Taskbar and select options such as SHOW CORTANA BUTTON or TASK VIEW BUTTON or TOUCH KEYBOARD BUTTON to change what appears in 2 and 7.

[Right Click] the Taskbar and select TASKBAR SETTINGS, then:

- Turn the various configuration options on or off. For example, choosing NEVER from the COMBINE TASKBAR BUTTONS list displays open Word files as separate Taskbar icons. This is a good choice if no more than 10 apps and files are open at any one time.
- [Click] SELECT WHICH ICONS APPEAR ON THE TASKBAR to modify the number of icons in 5 and 6.

The Taskbar behaves differently in Tablet mode (see **Working in Tablet Mode**). To change this behavior [Click] , then , SYSTEM, TABLET MODE.

Pinning an App to the Taskbar 3

1. [Right Click] any app on the Desktop, Taskbar (unpinned), or within the Start menu or, with File Explorer, an app or folder.
2. Select PIN TO TASKBAR.

To rearrange a pinned app, [Drag] it within the Taskbar.

Using Taskbar Jump Lists

[Swipe up] or [Right Click] a Taskbar button to display its Jump List.

Jump Lists show an app's recently used files, pinned files, and sometimes related tasks on the Taskbar.

Using the Action Center 7

1. [Click] (switches to if new messages are waiting) or [Swipe] in from the right screen edge to open the Action Center.
2. [Click] a message for details. To dismiss it, [Hover] and [Click] .

- [Click] CLEAR ALL NOTIFICATIONS to remove all messages.
- [Click] COLLAPSE to see more messages. The Quick Action button grid will collapse to a single row.

Power user tip: To configure the Quick Action buttons, [Click] , then , SYSTEM, NOTIFICATIONS & ACTIONS. Under QUICK ACTIONS, [Click] EDIT YOUR QUICK ACTIONS then [Drag] each button to the new position. Only the top row of buttons will display in Collapsed mode. [Click] + Add to add a button; [Click] the pin on any button to remove it.

Quick Actions include:

Tablet mode – see **Working in Tablet Mode**.

Focus Assist – Choose which notifications to receive.

Nearby sharing – turn NFC on/off.

All Settings – Opens the global settings app for Windows 10 (see **Settings & Troubleshooting**).

Top 10 Things You Need to Know

1. Sync all your computers, tablets, and smartphones so they look and act the same. You must use a single sign-in to sync your settings across all these devices. See **Starting Windows** as well as **Using the Settings App**.
2. Get to know Tablet mode if you have a tablet or smartphone. It behaves differently than Desktop mode. See **Working in Tablet Mode** as well as **Using the Touch Keyboard**.
3. The Start menu serves as the starting point for most of your device's activity. It is an essential element of Windows, functioning both as a list and launchpad for apps installed on your device. See **Accessing Apps and Content** to understand how it works.
4. All apps are windowed with a menu, title bar and close button. See how to manipulate them in **Working with Apps**.
5. Multiple desktops are used to visually arrange many running apps into logical groups. See **Working with Multiple Desktops**.
6. Access your documents through an appropriate app. Or use File Explorer by pressing <-E> or [Clicking] on the Taskbar.
7. File Explorer opens to the Quick Access view. Learn how to adjust its behavior with **Managing Content with File Explorer**.
8. Searching with Cortana, Microsoft's voice-activated virtual assistant, has been improved. Cortana can be used to search not only local files but the OneDrive cloud, Microsoft Store, and the web. It can also set reminders, dictate then send emails, and launch apps. See **Searching with Cortana**.
9. All app, settings and system notifications appear in a single place – the Action Center. They appear in a vertical list on the right edge. See **Using the Action Center**.
10. The default web browser is Microsoft Edge . See Beezix's **Edge & Internet Explorer 11** guide for details. You can find the Internet Explorer app via Search.

Windows 10 Shortcuts

Navigation

Open/Close Start menu (In Tablet mode switches between Start and last accessed app)	⊞ or Ctrl-Esc
Task View	⊞ - Tab or Swipe from Left
Cycle among open apps/windows	Alt/Alt-Shift - Tab
Cycle among Taskbar items	⊞ - T/⊞ - Shift-T
Cycle among open windows in the order they were opened (not in Tablet mode)	Alt-Esc
Cycle among elements in a window or dialog box	Tab/Shift-Tab or F6

Launching Apps

Open File Explorer	⊞ - E
Open the Action Center	⊞ - A
Open or select a Taskbar item	⊞ - number
Open the Run dialog	⊞ - R
Launch app as Administrator	Ctrl-Shift-Click
Close current window or open shutdown dialog	Alt - F4
Start Dictation	⊞ - H

Search

Search by typing or speaking	⊞ - S
Search within an open app	Ctrl - F
Search for, then connect to wireless devices	⊞ - K

Settings

All Settings	⊞ - I

Options

Context menu	[Right Click] or [Press and hold]
Power user tools	⊞ - X

Screens

Second Screen options	⊞ - P
Lock computer	⊞ - L
Zoom in and out	Ctrl-Mouse scroll wheel, or [Pinch/Stretch]
Show Desktop, Minimize/Restore all windows (not in Tablet mode)	⊞ - D

Screenshots

Capture a screenshot to both clipboard and Pictures/Screenshots folder	⊞ - PrtScn
Capture a screenshot of active window to both clipboard and Pictures/Screenshots folder	⊞ - Alt-PrtScn

App Windows

Restore, move, size, minimize/maximize close active window	Alt - Space
Cycle app window to each Snap quadrant (not in Tablet mode)	⊞ - Arrow
Move the current window/app from one monitor to the next	⊞ - Shift-← or →

Virtual Desktops (not in Tablet mode)

Create new Desktop	⊞ - Ctrl-D
Close current Desktop	⊞ - Ctrl-F4
Switch Desktops	⊞ - Ctrl-← or →

Help

Launch web help query	⊞ - F1
Help for active window	F1
Windows Task Manager	Ctrl-Shift-Esc

Working with Apps

Windows 10 features two app types. Desktop apps such as Notepad are not optimized for touch, have small controls and many menus. Windows apps such as Edge are optimized for touch with large controls and fewer menus. Windows apps either come with Windows or can be downloaded from the Store. Many require a Microsoft Account sign-in.

Starting an App

1. [Click] ⊞ 1 or press <⊞>.
2. [Click] an app to launch it.

- On the Taskbar, [Click] a pinned program.
- On the Desktop, [Double Click] a program shortcut.

For more about finding apps and settings, see **Searching for Apps**.

Opening an App File (Document)

1. Press <⊞-E>. Or, on the Taskbar, [Click] (see **Managing Content with File Explorer**).
2. [Double Click] to open a folder or library.
3. Locate then [Double Click] a file.

For a file that can be opened by multiple programs, choose a program by [Right Clicking] the file icon, choose OPEN WITH, then select from the list.

Saving an App File

Press <Ctrl-S> or choose FILE, SAVE to save changes to an existing file.

If saving a file for the first time or saving a copy to a new location:

1. Choose FILE, SAVE AS.
2. Choose a file location then enter a FILE NAME. A file name and location can be up to 256 characters in length. Do not use / \ : * ? " < > or ¦ .
3. [Click] SAVE.

Switching Between Windows/Apps

Taskbar buttons indicate which programs are open, have multiple windows, or need attention.

Closed	Open	Current Window	Multiple Windows	Needs Attention

- To activate an open app [Click] its Taskbar icon. If necessary, select from the list or thumbnails of open windows. To preview a window, [Hover] over a thumbnail.
- To cycle through active apps, hold <Alt> and press <Tab> repeatedly.

Switching with Task View

Task View zooms out the desktop view to display all currently running apps in miniature. It also displays a timeline of previously launched content. [Click] a displayed item to launch or switch to it.

1. Hold <⊞> and press <Tab>, or [Click] 2 or [Swipe] from the left screen edge.
2. [Click] an item.

Snapping Multiple Apps to the Same Screen

1. Press <⊞-← or →> on an open app to snap it to the left or right side of the screen. Alternatively, [Drag] the title bar to the left or right screen edge and release when the mouse pointer reaches the edge.
2. A subsequent press of the <⊞-↑ or ↓> snaps it to the upper or lower quadrant making room for up to four apps on the same screen.

- Windows will display thumbnails of other open apps in an empty quadrant. [Click] one and it will snap to a different screen quadrant.

Resizing an App

1. [Point] to an edge or corner of a non-full screen window. The mouse pointer changes to a double-headed arrow ⟺.
2. [Drag] the edge of the window.

Expand a window to full height: [Double Click] the top or bottom edge or press <⊞-Shift-↑>.

Moving an App

[Drag] an app by its title bar, avoiding the buttons.

Maximizing an App

Press <⊞-↑> on an open app or [Double Click] its title bar.

When a window is maximized, the Maximize button ☐ changes to a Restore button ❐.

Restoring to Previous Size

- [Double Click] the title bar.
- [Click] ❐.
- Press <⊞-↓>

Hiding an App

- [Click] ─, or press <⊞-↓> (twice if maximized).
- To minimize all open windows other than the current window, press <⊞-Home>.
- To minimize all open windows and show the Desktop, press <⊞-M>.

Closing an App

- Press <Alt-F4>.
- [Click] the app's Close button ✕.
- Choose FILE, CLOSE or FILE, EXIT from the app's menu bar or Ribbon.

Closing an App Window from the Taskbar

- [Hover] over a Taskbar button, then [Click] a thumbnail's ✕ button. In most cases, closing the last window closes an app.
- [Right Click] a Taskbar button then choose CLOSE WINDOW / ALL WINDOWS.

Searching for Apps

- With the Start menu open, just start typing.
- On the Taskbar, [Click] search icon, then type.
- Press <⊞-Q>, then type.

Select a category to restrict the search to local apps, settings, documents, etc. To switch to external results [Click] WEB.

See **Searching in File Explorer** for file and folder searches.

Tip: To show/hide the Taskbar's search icon, [Right Click] the Taskbar, [Click] SEARCH, then choose SHOW SEARCH ICON, SHOW SEARCH BOX, or HIDDEN.

Searching with Cortana

Cortana is Windows 10's speech-enabled virtual assistant. It responds to your natural language search requests and commands (requires embedded or attached microphone). It can also list notifications on command (calendar, email, etc.)

- [Click] ○ 2 then type your question or request.
- Speak the phrase "Hey Cortana" or [Click] ○ 2 then [Click] 🎤 in the pane's lower right, then ask your question. Using speech must first be enabled, see below.

Enable Speech Recognition: [Click] ⊞ then ⚙. [Click] PRIVACY, then SPEECH, then set ONLINE SPEECH RECOGNITION to ON.

Cortana Settings:

1. [Click] the Cortana icon ○ 2 then [Click] the Menu at the top left and choose SETTINGS. Sign in first, if necessary.
2. [Click] KEYBOARD SHORTCUT to use the <⊞-C> shortcut to activate Cortana.
3. [Click] MICROPHONE to enable/disable microphone use and speech recognition.
4. [Click] VOICE ACTIVATION to adjust permissions. Toggle LET CORTANA RESPOND TO "CORTANA" KEYWORD and USE CORTANA EVEN WHEN MY DEVICE IS LOCKED as desired.

Working with Multiple Desktops

If you have many open apps, but not multiple monitors, you can organize them into multiple virtual Desktops.

1. Go to Task View.
2. At the top, [Click] NEW DESKTOP ＋.
3. [Click] the new Desktop thumbnail, then open apps as necessary.

- Each Desktop's Taskbar displays its own set of icons for open apps.
  To change this [Click] ⊞, then ⚙, SYSTEM, MULTITASKING, VIRTUAL DESKTOPS.
- To move open apps from one Desktop to another switch to Task View 2, [Right Click] an app window, [Click] MOVE TO then select the destination Desktop.

Managing Content with File Explorer

Managing Files and Folders

Press <⊞-E> or [Click] on the Taskbar to start File Explorer.

- The **Ribbon** 8 provides options and tools to work with files and folders. Some Ribbon tabs are specific to a file type, e.g., MANAGE, PICTURE TOOLS only appears if an image file is selected.

  [Click] a Ribbon tab (HOME, VIEW, etc.) to open it. Or, press <Alt> then press the indicated letter.

  [Right Click] a Ribbon tab and deselect MINIMIZE THE RIBBON or [Click] 9 to permanently expand the Ribbon.
- The **Navigation Pane** on the left displays your available folders and drives. The right side **Content Pane** displays the selected folder's files. To change what is displayed, choose VIEW, NAVIGATION PANE then:

  EXPAND TO OPEN FOLDER: Show folders in the Navigation Pane as you open them on the right.

  SHOW ALL FOLDERS: Show folders normally hidden, such as Control Panel and Recycle Bin.
- The **Preview Pane** previews the content of certain files (documents, images, videos). To enable, choose VIEW, PREVIEW PANE.
- The **Details Pane** displays select file details such as size or availability. To enable choose VIEW, DETAILS PANE.

Customizing the Quick Access Toolbar 13

The Quick Access Toolbar displays icons for frequently used Ribbon commands. To add a command:

1. [Click] ▾, then [Click] a command.

Navigating in File Explorer

- In the Navigation Pane [Click] a folder to see its contents on the right.
- See subfolders or hide them by moving the mouse into the Navigation Pane, then [Clicking] › or ⌄.
- In the Address Bar 10, [Click] a folder name, or [Click] › to its right to jump to its subfolder.
- In the Content pane, [Double Click] a drive or folder.

To navigate between already viewed folders: [Click] ← or → 11. [Click] ⌄ to select from a list of folders or ↑ to move up one folder level to its parent.

Customizing the Default Quick Access View

Quick Access, the default view for File Explorer, automatically displays frequently or recently visited files or folders.

1. [Click] VIEW, OPTIONS.
2. To change the default view, from the OPEN FILE EXPLORER TO list, choose THIS PC.
3. In the Privacy section, toggle checkboxes for SHOW RECENTLY USED FILES IN QUICK ACCESS and SHOW FREQUENTLY USED FOLDERS IN QUICK ACCESS to disable the automatic display of frequent and recent items.

To add or remove Quick Access items, [Right Click] the item, then select PIN TO QUICK ACCESS or REMOVE or UNPIN FROM QUICK ACCESS.

Searching in File Explorer

1. Navigate to a folder then [Click] 12 or press <Ctrl-F>.
2. Enter your search term. Matching file/folder names or file contents automatically display in the Content pane.

Refining Your Search

[Click] 12 or press <Ctrl-F> to see the SEARCH TOOLS, SEARCH Ribbon tab.

- THIS PC to search the entire computer, CURRENT FOLDER to only search the current folder, ALL SUBFOLDERS to search all subfolders of the selected folder, and SEARCH AGAIN IN to search a recent location.
- Select DATE MODIFIED, KIND, or SIZE as additional criteria.
- Select OTHER PROPERTIES, NAME to only search for the file name.

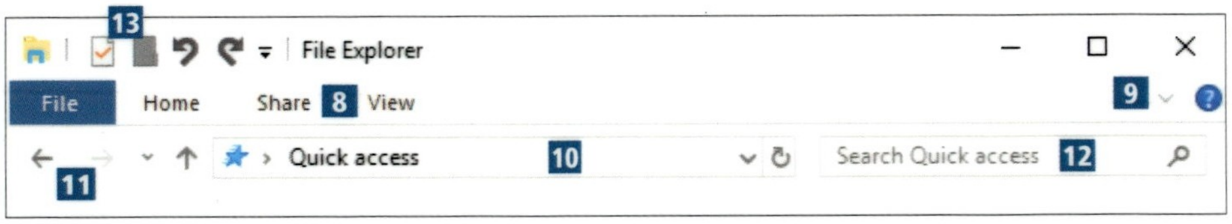

Changing File Explorer's Display

Choose VIEW, then [Hover] over options in the LAYOUT group to preview changes. [Click] to select a new view.

Power user tip: To add more columns to the DETAILS view choose VIEW, ADD COLUMNS, and select additional columns to display. Or, [Right Click] any column heading, and select additional columns.

Grouping Files and Folders

To keep files and folders together based on criteria such as date (today, yesterday), file type (pictures, spreadsheets), or size, choose VIEW, GROUP BY then select a grouping.

Sorting Files and Folders

Choose VIEW, SORT BY, then a method.

Opening a Second Explorer Window

Press <⊞-E> or [Right Click] the folder and choose OPEN IN NEW WINDOW.

Creating a Folder

1. Navigate to the location for the new folder.
2. Choose HOME, then NEW FOLDER.
3. Type a folder name. Press <Enter>.

Renaming Files or Folders

1. Select the folder or file you wish to rename.
2. Press <F2> or choose HOME, RENAME.
3. Type a new name, then press <Enter>.

Selecting Multiple Items

- [Drag] across a group of items.
- Adjacent items: [Click] the first item, then press <Shift> while [Clicking] the last item.
- Non-adjacent items: [Click] one item, then press <Ctrl> while [Clicking] other items.
- All items: Choose HOME, Select all or press <Ctrl-A>.
- To select everything but what is currently selected: Choose HOME, Invert selection.
- De-select an item: Press <Ctrl> while [Clicking] an item.
- De-select all items: [Click] a blank area or choose HOME, Select none.

Selecting Items with Checkboxes

- Enable by choosing VIEW, ITEM CHECK BOXES.
- [Hover] over a file, folder, or library, then [Click] the checkbox to the left.

Deleting Files or Folders

1. Select item(s) to delete. Local items (including offline OneDrive® files or folders) are sent to the Recycle Bin. They can be restored if a mistake is made. Network items will be permanently deleted ([Click] YES when asked).
2. Press <Delete> or choose HOME, DELETE.

Restoring Deleted Items

1. [Double Click] the RECYCLE BIN on the Desktop, or select it within File Explorer.
2. Select the item(s) to restore.
3. To return item(s) to the original location, on the tab MANAGE, RECYCLE BIN TOOLS [Click] RESTORE THE SELECTED ITEMS. Or, [Drag] the item(s) to a different location.

Deleting Permanently

- Select an individual item. Choose HOME, then the drop-down of DELETE, then PERMANENTLY DELETE.
- For all items in the Recycle Bin: [Right Click] the RECYCLE BIN, and choose EMPTY RECYCLE BIN. [Click] YES.

Linking to a Document, Folder, or App

Create links to files or apps so they can be accessed from multiple locations. Icons for these shortcuts, display a small lower left arrow. Deleting a link does not delete the original.

- [Right Click] the original item, then choose CREATE SHORTCUT. [Drag] the shortcut to a new location. Or, to place a shortcut on the desktop, choose SEND TO then DESKTOP (CREATE SHORTCUT).
- [Right Drag] the item to a new location, release then choose CREATE SHORTCUTS HERE.
- Copy the item. [Right Click] on the destination, then choose PASTE SHORTCUT.

Moving and Copying Files and Folders

1. Select the file(s) and/or folder(s) to move or copy.
2. [Drag] to move or <Ctrl>-[Drag] to copy. Release the item over another folder, window, the Navigation Pane, or the Desktop. In the Navigation Pane, to see subfolders, while [Dragging], [Hover] over the parent folder.

   Or

   Choose HOME, MOVE TO, or COPY TO. Select a recent location or CHOOSE LOCATION, select a new location, then [Click] MOVE or COPY.

Using Cut, Copy & Paste for Files

1. Select file(s) and/or folder(s) to copy.
2. Press <Ctrl-C> or choose HOME, COPY. Or to move a file, press <Ctrl-X> or choose HOME, Cut.
3. Navigate to the destination folder.
4. Press <Ctrl-V> or choose HOME, PASTE.

Mouse/Touch Equivalents

Mouse	Touch
Click	Tap
Double Click	Double Tap
Right Click	Press and Hold, then release when a box appears
Drag	Drag

Other Touch Actions

- [Pinch/Stretch] Move two fingers towards each other or away to shrink/enlarge.
- [Rotate] With 2 or more fingers, turn your hand.
- [Swipe from Right/Left/Top/Bottom] Quickly move your finger starting from a screen edge.

Using the Touch Keyboard

Add On-Screen Keyboard to Taskbar: [Right Click] the Taskbar, select SHOW TOUCH KEYBOARD BUTTON.

Switch to On-Screen Keyboard: [Tap] an area to input text such as on a form.

Or, on the Taskbar, [Tap].

While typing, [Tap] a suggestion next to your text to insert it.

To switch between on-screen input types, [Tap] the on-screen input icon, then select another:

Keyboard	
Thumb Keyboard (better for holding a tablet)	
Handwriting	
Turn Caps Lock ON	[Double tap] ↑
One-handed Touch Keyboard	

Dock/Undock keyboard: to Dock, to Undock. When undocked, [Drag] top of undocked keyboard to reposition.

Sending Files and Folders (Zip)

Gather files and folders into a single compressed file then attach that file to a message.

1. Select the items to zip.
2. Choose SHARE, then ZIP .
3. Rename the zip file if desired, then press <Enter>.

The zip file appears as a folder in File Explorer and acts just like any other folder. You can select it, add files or folders to it, and delete items from it.

Unzipping (Extracting) Files

1. Select a zip folder.
2. Choose EXTRACT, COMPRESSED FOLDER TOOLS, then EXTRACT ALL .
3. [Click] BROWSE to find a destination folder.
4. [Click] EXTRACT.

Extract specific files:

1. Open a zip folder then select the items to extract.
2. Move or copy items as usual. Or, choose EXTRACT, COMPRESSED FOLDER TOOLS, then a frequently used location, or [Click] then CHOOSE LOCATION. [Click] COPY if necessary.

Working with Libraries

A convenient way to organize content that is widely spread but has a common purpose is to gather it into a single, convenient library. For example, links to scattered picture folders can be found in a single default Pictures library. Libraries created from folder links display the contents of those folders in one place when viewing the library.

- Windows 10 does not show libraries by default. To display them, open File Explorer and choose VIEW, NAVIGATION PANE, SHOW LIBRARIES.
- To view or manage libraries in File Explorer, [Click] Libraries in the Navigation Pane.
- To create a new library: [Right Click] a blank spot in the LIBRARIES folder, select NEW then LIBRARY. Type a name, then press <Enter>.
- To modify a library name, [Right Click] its name, select RENAME, then type a new name and press <Enter>.
- To add a folder link to a library, [Right Click] a folder in the Navigation Pane, select INCLUDE IN LIBRARY, then choose a library or [Click] CREATE NEW LIBRARY. You can add the same folder link to many libraries.
- To remove a folder from a library, navigate to the library then choose MANAGE, LIBRARY TOOLS, MANAGE LIBRARY . Select a folder, [Click] REMOVE, then OK.

  You may need to refresh the screen (press <F5>).
  This does not delete the original folder, only the library link.

Warning: The original folder contents will be affected by changes made to its library copy. For example, deleting a library file will also delete the original.

Working in Tablet Mode

Tablet mode transforms Windows 10 into a touch-friendly environment with a full-screen Start menu and full-screen apps.

Configuring Tablet Mode

1. [Click] , then , SYSTEM then TABLET.
2. Choose the sign-in mode, how to switch modes or [Click] CHANGE ADDITIONAL TABLET SETTINGS for more options

To quickly toggle Tablet Mode on or off, [Click] 7 to open the Taskbar's Action Center, then [Click] TABLET MODE.

Using Tablet Mode

- Return to the Start screen: [Tap] .
- Starting apps: Return to the Start screen and [Tap] an app tile or [Tap] in screen's top left then select app.
- To access system apps [Tap] then a sidebar icon (Account, File Explorer, Settings, Power).
- Switch between apps: [Swipe] in from the left screen edge or [Tap] on the Taskbar. You can also use to switch back to the Start screen.
- Closing apps: Perform a full [Drag] or [Swipe] from the screen top to the screen bottom.

Settings & Troubleshooting

Settings are distributed across two apps: Settings and Control Panel.

Using the Settings App

Adjust global settings, connected devices, wireless and network connections, privacy, system updates and more.

1. [Click] , then , or [Click] 7 then ALL SETTINGS or press <-I>.
2. [Click] the desired setting group, then choose a setting to modify from the list on the left.
3. [Click] top left ← to return to previous screen, or [Click] Home to return to main Settings screen.

Useful settings are:

NETWORK & INTERNET, WI-FI – to manage your Wi-Fi.

ACCOUNTS, YOUR INFO – to assign an account picture, and manage related accounts.

ACCOUNTS, SYNC YOUR SETTINGS – to sync passwords, themes and other Windows settings across all devices accessed with the same sign-in.

UPDATE & SECURITY, BACKUP – backup and restore files.

APPS, APPS & FEATURES – to uninstall, modify, or move an app.

APPS, DEFAULT APPS – to change which is the default app for email, music, etc.

APPS, OFFLINE MAPS – to download maps for offline directions.

Adding a Picture or Slide Show to Your Lock Screen

1. Within Settings, [Click] PERSONALIZATION, LOCK SCREEN.
2. Select PICTURE from the BACKGROUND list, then select a picture. Alternatively, [Click] BROWSE to select an image file.

To play a slide show instead:

1. Select SLIDESHOW, then [Click] ADD A FOLDER. Browse to, then select a folder for the slideshow then [Click] CHOOSE THIS FOLDER.

Setting Up Wi-Fi

1. Within Settings, [Click] NETWORK & INTERNET, WI-FI.
2. [Click] SHOW AVAILABLE NETWORKS. From the right side list [Click] a network, then [Click] CONNECT.
3. If necessary, enter the password.

Wi-Fi and Airplane mode can also be managed from the Action Center:

1. [Click] 7 to open the Taskbar's Action Center. If necessary, [Click] EXPAND to display more actions.
2. Select NETWORK then, [Click] the default Wi-Fi connection, or [Click] WI-FI to toggle it on/off.

Using Airplane Mode

To turn off all wireless communications:

1. [Click] 7.
2. [Click] AIRPLANE MODE to toggle it on/off.

Using the Control Panel App

Use to change advanced settings and device options.

1. Press <> then start typing "control panel".
2. [Click] the option once it appears.
3. [Click] a Control Panel option. Or if in CATEGORY view, [Click] a category heading to see all options for that category.

What to Try if an App Freezes

1. [Right Click] then select TASK MANAGER or press <Ctrl-Shift-Esc>.
2. If necessary, [Click] MORE DETAILS.
3. If an app's STATUS is blank, wait a short time to see if the program unfreezes. If the STATUS is NOT RESPONDING, select the program and [Click] END TASK.

Getting Help

[Click] 2, type your question, then press <Enter>. The answer will be found via a web search, so tailor your query accordingly.

Users & Security

Changing Users

Each user should have their own sign-in to make personal files and settings inaccessible to others.

- On the sign-in screen: To sign in as another user [Click] a different user name in the bottom left corner. Sign in as usual.
- On the desktop: To switch to another user [Click] , then [Click] , choose a different user then sign in as usual.

Adding User Sign-Ins

Only available to local administrator account users. [Click] , then , ACCOUNTS, FAMILY & OTHER USERS then:

1. [Click] ADD A FAMILY MEMBER or ADD SOMEONE ELSE TO THIS PC.
2. Enter their email address then [Click] NEXT.
3. [Click] CONFIRM then CLOSE. An invitation is sent to the email address.

If they don't have an email address, create an Outlook.com one for them.

1. For an adult, [Click] ADD SOMEONE ELSE TO THIS PC.
2. [Click] I DON'T HAVE THIS PERSON'S SIGN IN INFORMATION. [Click] GET A NEW EMAIL ADDRESS.
3. Enter the user's NEW EMAIL.
4. Enter a PASSWORD (must be at least 8 characters and contain at least two of uppercase, lower case, number or symbol characters) then [Click] NEXT.
5. Modify settings, [Click] NEXT then CLOSE.

1. Or for a child, [Click] ADD A FAMILY MEMBER, then [Click] CREATE ONE FOR A CHILD.
2. Enter the NEW EMAIL and PASSWORD, [Clicking] NEXT after each entry.
3. Enter name, location and birth date information. Permissions wil be set according to the age selected.
4. [Click] CLOSE when finished.

If you don't want to create an OTHER USER email address, create a local Login for use on a single device:

1. [Click] ADD SOMEONE ELSE TO THIS PC.
2. [Click] I DON'T HAVE THIS PERSON'S SIGN-IN INFO.
3. [Click] ADD A USER WITHOUT A MICROSOFT ACCOUNT.
4. Enter the new USER NAME, PASSWORD twice, then up to 3 SECURITY QUESTIONS and answers. [Click] NEXT.

Configuring Sign-In

1. [Click] , then , ACCOUNTS, SIGN-IN OPTIONS.
2. [Click] an option to CHANGE or ADD, including PIN, PASSWORD, PICTURE PASSWORD, SECURITY KEY, and WINDOWS HELLO FACE or FINGERPRINT, if available.
3. If prompted, confirm your new setting, then [Click] OK.
   - Password: Type current, then new password twice.
   - PIN: Enter the current, then new PIN twice.
   - Picture password:
     a. Enter password if asked then [Click] CHOOSE PICTURE.
     b. Locate and choose a picture. [Click] OPEN.
     c. [Click] USE THIS PICTURE.
     d. Draw 3 circles/lines/dots, then repeat when prompted, with same size, position, and direction.
4. [Click] NEXT and/or FINISH.

ISBN 978-1-944684-51-8